PAUSING TO PRAY
Lenten Meditations for Busy People

With Excerpts from the *Diary of St. Faustina* and
Meditations by Marian Fathers of the Immaculate Conception

Compiled and arranged by Sarah M. Chichester

D1444419

MARIAN PRESS
STOCKBRIDGE MA 01263

2010

Available from:
Marian Helpers Center
Stockbridge, MA 01263

Prayerline:1-800-804-3823
Orderline: 1-800-462-7426
Website: www.marian.org

Imprimi Potest:
Very Rev. Daniel Cambra, MIC
Provincial Superior
The Blessed Virgin Mary, Mother of Mercy Province
October 21, 2010

ISBN: 978-1-59614-233-6

Design and Layout: Curtis Bohner
Cover Photo: Felix Carroll

For texts from the English Edition of
Diary of St. Maria Faustina Kowalska:

Nihil Obstat:
George H. Pearce, SM
Former Archbishop of Suva, Fiji

Imprimatur:
Joseph F. Maguire
Bishop of Springfield, MA
April 9, 1984

Printed in the United States of America

In order to hear the voice of God, one has to have silence in one's soul and to keep silence; not a gloomy silence, but an interior silence; that is to say, recollection in God. One can speak a great deal without breaking silence and, on the contrary, one can speak little and be constantly breaking silence. … God does not give Himself to a chattering soul which, like a drone in a beehive, buzzes around but gathers no honey. A talkative soul is empty inside (118).

Meditation:
Dear Jesus, sometimes I am afraid of silence. I fill my day with distractions, with music, with background noise, and with other things because I fear the void. Maybe I am afraid of what You will ask of me. Help me to not be afraid of silence. Help me to realize that, in Your gentleness, You will never force Your will on me. Teach me how to open my heart to You, so I can receive what it is that You want to give me. Help me to find You in the silence.

Jesus, I Trust In You

Thursday after Ash Wednesday

Meditation by Fr. Joseph Roesch, MIC

O my Jesus, I will console You for all the ingratitude, the blasphemies, the coldness, the hatred of the wicked, the sacrileges (80).

Meditation:
My Lord, I really do love You! I am not always very good at demonstrating this through my actions. I want to remain close to you in reparation for those who are against You and who break Your Heart in this way. As You said from the Cross, they do not know what they are doing. I will love You for them, to make up for the lack of love in their hearts. In this way, I hope to also win graces for their conversion. For if they truly knew You, how could they not love You?

Jesus, I Trust In You

Friday after Ash Wednesday

Meditation by Fr. Joseph Roesch, MIC

I desire that you know more profoundly the love that burns in My Heart for souls, and you will understand this when you meditate on My Passion (186).

Meditation:

Lord, it is true that I don't realize the depth of Your burning love for souls. I know that the great saints would often meditate on Your Cross, but I have been afraid to do so. I have thought that it would be too depressing or overwhelming. I will ask Our Lady to help me not to run away from Your Cross as I have done. I will remain with You and meditate on Your Passion, which You underwent for my sake. Set my heart on fire with a burning love like Yours, O Jesus!

Jesus, I Trust In You

Saturday after Ash Wednesday

Meditation by Fr. Joseph Roesch, MIC

Although it seems to me that You do not hear me, I put my trust in the ocean of Your mercy, and I know that my hope will not be deceived (69).

Meditation:

My Jesus, when I repeatedly ask You for something and I get no reply and nothing seems to change in my life, I fear that You are not there. I grow discouraged and I feel alone. Help me to trust in You in the midst of the darkness. Teach me how to walk by faith and not by sight. I place my hope in You, and I believe that Your love and mercy are as deep as the ocean. There is nothing that is beyond Your power. Strengthen my faith, O Lord!

Jesus, I Trust In You

Tell sinners that no one shall escape My Hand; if they run away from My Merciful Heart, they will fall into My Just Hands. Tell sinners that I am always waiting for them, that I listen intently to the beating of their heart ... when will it beat for Me? (1728).

Meditation:

Dear Jesus, it is hard to trust in Your words. They seem too good to be true! I know that I am a sinner and that I don't deserve Your mercy. I have ignored You for so long, how can You be so good as to wait for me to come around and to turn back to You? I want to be good, and I want to believe in Your goodness. Help me, O Lord, to trust. Help me to change my ways so that I am no longer afraid of You, and can just love You!

Jesus, I Trust In You

First Monday of Lent
Meditation by Fr. Joseph Roesch, MIC

Although My greatness is beyond understanding, I commune only with those who are little. I demand of you a childlike spirit (332).

Meditation:
My Savior, I remember how I depended on my parents for everything when I was young. I took all that they did for me for granted. I now realize how deep their love has always been for me. Teach me how to depend on You with a childlike trust. I know it will take all eternity for me to begin to comprehend your greatness. But I can begin today. Little by little, I can grow in my appreciation of You and in my love for You!

Jesus, I Trust In You

First Tuesday of Lent
Meditation by Fr. Joseph Roesch, MIC

My daughter, suffering will be a sign to you that I am with you (669).

Meditation:
Dear Jesus, I have always been afraid of suffering. I don't like pain of any kind, and I fear being abandoned and alone. Teach me to trust that You won't abandon me in the midst of my suffering, but that my suffering is a sign that You are with me in a special way. My Lord, help me to trust in this truth and to not run away from trials. Help me to realize that You are always very close to me, and never more so than when I am in the midst of some type of suffering.

Jesus, I Trust In You

First Wednesday of Lent

Meditation by Fr. Joseph Roesch, MIC

When we pray, we ought not force the Lord God to give us what we want, but we should rather submit to His holy will (1525).

Meditation:

Dear Jesus, I know that St. Faustina once wrote the words "My will" on a page in her *Diary* and then she crossed them out because she only wanted to do Your will. I am afraid to let go of my will, Lord. I am afraid that I will not be happy if I am not able to do my own will. I am sorry that I try to force You to do my will, Lord. Teach me how to surrender. Take away my fear and help me to be more like St. Faustina.

Jesus, I Trust In You

First Thursday of Lent
Meditation by Fr. Joseph Roesch, MIC

I was reflecting on how much God had suffered and on how great was the love He had shown for us, and on the fact that we still do not believe that God loves us so much. O Jesus, who can understand this? What suffering it is for our Savior! How can He convince us of His love if even His death cannot convince us? (319).

Meditation:
My Savior, it is so easy for me to fall into the trap of the Evil One and to believe that You don't love me. When the trials come, the thought that You don't care about me always comes into my head. How quickly I forget all that You endured for me. I am sorry, Jesus! I want to keep the image of Your Cross near me always so that I will never forget Your love for me. Give me the grace to believe in Your great love for me, even in the midst of my trials.

Jesus, I Trust In You

First Friday of Lent
Meditation by Fr. Joseph Roesch, MIC

I saw how the Lord Jesus suffered as He was being scourged. Oh, such an inconceivable agony! How terribly Jesus suffered during the scourging! O poor sinners, on the day of judgment how will you face the Jesus whom you are now torturing so cruelly: His blood flowed to the ground, and in some places His flesh started to fall off. I saw a few bare bones on His back. The meek Jesus moaned softly and sighed (188).

Meditation:
My Lord, how selfish I am sometimes. I only care about my own ease and comfort. I forget about the suffering of others in the world, and I rarely think about all that You suffered on my behalf. I don't think about how my sins contributed to Your suffering. My Jesus, I ask for the grace of a conversion of heart. I don't want to offend You, I want to comfort You, and to love You. Thank You for Your great love for me!

Jesus, I Trust In You

First Saturday of Lent

Meditation by Fr. Joseph Roesch, MIC

Jesus, I accept everything that You wish to send me; I trust in Your goodness (190).

Meditation:

Dear Jesus, I am afraid of what I would have to give up if I gave You my unconditional "Yes." I guess I don't trust You enough. How did St. Faustina come to a complete surrender to You? She knew You better than I do. Help me to come to know You more deeply, Lord. I don't want to be afraid of the path that You have picked out for me. Help me to believe that You will be with me every step of the way and that my surrender to You won't lead to misery, but is the key to my happiness.

Jesus, I Trust In You

O my Jesus, keep me near to You! See how weak I am! I cannot go a step forward by myself; so You, Jesus, must stand by me constantly like a mother by a helpless child — and even more so (264).

Meditation:

Jesus, you know what happens when *I* rely on myself, when *I* take charge of my life. I make a mess of everything, and I hurt the people I love and who love me. So, Jesus, today, *You* take charge of my life, *You* guide me constantly. I surrender my life to You.

Jesus, I Trust In You

Second Monday of Lent
Meditation by Fr. Donald Calloway, MIC

The Lord, so very great though He is, delights in humble souls. The more a soul humbles itself, the greater the kindness with which the Lord approaches it (1092).

Meditation:
Today, Lord, I am very aware of my limitations, my weaknesses, my sins. And I bring them all to You. I trust in Your love for me.

Jesus, I Trust In You

Second Tuesday of Lent
Meditation by Fr. Donald Calloway, MIC

In difficult moments, I will fix my gaze upon the silent Heart of Jesus, stretched upon the Cross, and from the exploding flames of His merciful Heart, will flow down upon me power and strength to keep fighting (906).

Meditation:

When I am tired or discouraged, I look to You, Jesus, to Your merciful Heart and Your immense love for me. In Your love, You left me Yourself in the Eucharist. In it, I find the hidden strength to continue this battle for my soul and for all souls. Refresh me. Transform me. Sustain me. I look to You, O Lord.

Jesus, I Trust In You

Second Wednesday of Lent

Meditation by Fr. Donald Calloway, MIC

At that moment Jesus asked me, **My child, how is your retreat going?** I answered, "But Jesus, You know how it is going." **Yes, I know, but I want to hear it from your own lips and from your heart** (295).

Meditation:

It seems kind of crazy that You, Jesus, want me to tell You about my day and about myself — You know everything! But it's so important to You that I talk to You, that I include You in my day, even in seemingly unimportant things. Help me to open my heart to You and to trust that You are always there waiting to hear from me.

Jesus, I Trust In You

Second Thursday of Lent

Meditation by Fr. Donald Calloway, MIC

The loss of each soul plunges Me into mortal sadness. You always console Me when you pray for sinners. The prayer most pleasing to Me is prayer for the conversion of sinners. Know, My daughter, that this prayer is always heard and answered (1397).

Meditation:

How great is the power of prayer! Let us always pray for the conversion of sinners, especially unrepentant sinners who are dying. Hear our prayers, Lord. We trust in You, that our prayers are always answered, in Your way, and in Your time.

Jesus, I Trust In You

Second Friday of Lent

Meditation by Fr. Donald Calloway, MIC

I saw the suffering Savior. What struck me was that Jesus was so peaceful amidst His great sufferings. I understood that this was a lesson for me on what my outward behavior should be in the midst of my various sufferings (1467).

Meditation:

Lord, how often do I complain when things don't go right, when my plans fall through, when I'm misunderstood, or persecuted? Instead of grumbling, let my heart offer You a simple sacrifice of praise. Praise You, Jesus, for this little gift of suffering that I can offer up to You.

Jesus, I Trust In You

Second Saturday of Lent

Meditation by Fr. Donald Calloway, MIC

Most Holy Trinity, I trust in Your infinite mercy. God is my Father and so I, His child, have every claim to His divine Heart; and the greater the darkness, the more complete our trust should be (357).

Meditation:
Father, wherever You send me, I will go. Whatever You want me to do, I will do. I won't rely on myself, but on You, Lord, and I will never be disappointed. Even though my path may seem dark and my duty impossible; nevertheless, I trust in You.

Jesus, I Trust In You

You are my great joy; your love and your humility make Me leave the heavenly throne and unite Myself with you. Love fills up the abyss that exists between My greatness and your nothingness (512).

Meditation:

Help me, Lord Jesus. Help me to do Your will. As you can see, my work and my prayer, even my love, all that I offer you, is like the feeble cry of a little one. Be my Love and my Strength. Ah, to be Your joy! You love me to folly, dear Jesus. Let me rest in Your love today, Lord, so that I don't forget that I am Your joy and You are my everything.

Jesus, I Trust In You

Third Monday of Lent
Meditation by Fr. Leszek Czeluśniak, MIC

Oh, how good the Lord is in not letting me go astray! I know that He will guard me, even jealously, but only as long as I remain little, because it is with such that the great Lord likes to commune. As to proud souls, He watches them from afar and opposes them (1440).

Meditation:
Today, I am afraid of nothing. I am not afraid of my littleness. I am not afraid of my falls. For as many times as I fall today, I will turn to You — not discouraged, but with a contrite heart. I will tell You everything. To convert means to turn around to You, to face You, to look toward You, to love You with all my energy, my mind, my soul, and my heart. Jesus, I beg You for the grace to be continually converted today, to begin yet again in seeking You, no matter how many times I have to turn back to You.

Jesus, I Trust In You

Third Tuesday of Lent
Meditation by Fr. Leszek Czeluśniak, MIC

Oh, if only the suffering soul knew how it is loved by God, it would die of joy and excess of happiness! Some day, we will know the value of suffering, but then we will no longer be able to suffer. The present moment is ours (963).

Meditation:
Jesus, You are my great Teacher. From You, I learn the value of suffering. From You, I learn how to recognize all of the little and big crosses that You give to me today. Increase my awareness of my daily crosses, so that I may offer them back to You, especially for poor sinners. Sometimes my path to You is full of sharp rocks and pebbles. But, when I pick them up and give them to Mary, she cleans them off and underneath the dirt and grime is a jewel. Even though I have trouble seeing the jewel, please take these crosses, these jewels, of mine and, through the hands of Mary, may they shine brilliantly before You. Let me not overlook one cross today, but may I offer each one to You with joy.

Jesus, I Trust In You

Third Wednesday of Lent

Meditation by Fr. Leszek Czeluśniak, MIC

I spend every free moment at the feet of the hidden God. He is my Master; I ask Him about everything; I speak to Him about everything. Here I obtain strength and light; here I learn everything; here I am given light on how to act toward my neighbor (704).

Meditation:

What can I do for You, Lord Jesus? What can *I* do? I am really a small one. How can my life change anything? And yet, in some mysterious way, my life can change the world. Through intercessory prayer, I can touch people all over the world. You are God and I am a creature, yet You ask me to seek You out, to converse with You, to ask You for anything. No petition is too small for You or too difficult for You. Today, Jesus, let me remember those I love who are far from You. I beg Your graces upon them. My trust is in You, O Lord.

Jesus, I Trust In You

Third Thursday of Lent

Meditation by Fr. Leszek Czeluśniak, MIC

I do not fear anything in the world, but fear only lest I make Jesus sad (610).

Meditation:

What is most important? Jesus, You created me in love. You redeemed me with Your Blood. Then why am I so full of fear? My life is ruled by fear of failure, fear of what others think, fear of losing the love of those around me, fear of being forgotten, or fear of being lonely. In the past, I've resisted giving You these fears. The most important thing in my life is loving You, so I freely give You these fears. Today I will look for ways to put You first. If I start to worry again, I will stop, give it to You, and then continue my day. May my constant acts of trust and surrender bring You joy.

Jesus, I Trust In You

Third Friday of Lent

Meditation by Fr. Leszek Czeluśniak, MIC

And when it seems to you that your suffering exceeds your strength, contemplate My wounds, and you will rise above human scorn and judgment. Meditation on My Passion will help you rise above all things (1184).

Meditation:

What do I have to do? What is my mission, my vocation? I have to look for Your will, Jesus. You want to show me that Your plan and Your provisions are the best things I could ever have. Your life, dear Jesus, is my best example: You came to do the will of the Father, that was Your mission. Such a difficult mission! Yet You prayed for the Father's will, "Thy will be done on earth as it is in heaven." When my crosses seem more than I can bear, let me look to You with trust and echo, "Thy will be done."

Jesus, I Trust In You

Third Saturday of Lent

Meditation by Fr. Leszek Czeluśniak, MIC

O my God, my only hope, I have placed all my trust in You, and I know I shall not be disappointed (317).

Meditation:

There is only one source of true happiness in my life: to accept Your love and love You in return. You created me. You seek me out. You will never, not even for a second, abandon me. Why such love for me? I cannot repay You in the slightest. So let me love You. May my love for You come forth in my trust and in my thanks. I thank You, Jesus, for Yourself in the Holy Eucharist, the greatest gift that I can receive in this life, for my life, for my crosses, for my future, wherever it may lead me. Thank You. My life is in Your hands. I have placed all my trust in You.

Jesus, I Trust In You

Fourth Sunday of Lent
Meditation by Fr. Michael Gaitley, MIC

There is no misery that could be a match for My mercy, neither will misery exhaust it, because as it is being granted — it increases. The soul that trusts in My mercy is most fortunate, because I Myself take care of it (1273).

Meditation:

Thank You, Jesus, for Your merciful Heart. I trust in Your mercy, and I happily accept Your special care. But when I begin to feel anxious or discouraged and my trust falters, I beg You, please don't abandon me. Instead, give me the grace to trust in You completely. Jesus, I trust You to do this. After all, isn't my misery greatest during those times of darkness? And didn't You just say, "There is no misery that could be a match for My mercy?" Well, then, I know Your mercy will be there for me during those trials. Thank You, Jesus, for Your mercy, which reaches out to me, especially in the darkness.

Jesus, I Trust In You

Fourth Monday of Lent
Meditation by Fr. Michael Gaitley, MIC

The more I come to know the greatness of God, the more joyful I become that He is as He is. And I rejoice immensely in His greatness and am delighted that I am so little because, since I am little, He carries me in His arms and holds me close to His Heart (779).

Meditation:
My God, what am I compared to You? You are Wisdom, I am foolishness. You are Almighty, I am weak. You are all Good, I am full of sin. But none of this discourages me, because You are my Father, and I am Your child. Your grace sustains me and gives me courage to go to You and accept Your mercy. If You were not my Father, I would be full of terror. But You have chosen me as Your own, and I rejoice in Your goodness and love.

Jesus, I Trust In You

Fourth Tuesday of Lent

Meditation by Fr. Michael Gaitley, MIC

I do not ask, Lord, that You take me down from the cross, but I implore You to give me the strength to remain steadfast upon it (1484).

Meditation:

Lord, St. Faustina is a great saint. I'm not. Sometimes I complain about even the littlest crosses in my life. Well, as You gave Faustina the grace to accept her big crosses, please give me the grace not to complain about my little ones. You are so merciful that You forget what a complainer I've been. Today, Lord, I begin again. Out of love for You, I will try to give You a smile when I feel the splinters from the Cross. And if I have to begin again tomorrow, I won't get discouraged. After all, You love little souls most especially, and I'm certainly much smaller than Faustina.

Jesus, I Trust In You

Fourth Wednesday of Lent

Meditation by Fr. Michael Gaitley, MIC

In the evening, I went in for a long talk with the Lord Jesus. ... I poured out my whole heart before Him, all my troubles, fears and apprehensions. Jesus lovingly listened to me and then said, **Be at peace, My child, I am with you** (1674).

Meditation:

Dear Jesus, how often I forget to speak with You! Here You are, with me all the time. You're in my heart and pervade my being, and Your beauty fills the earth. So why do I so often forget You? Well, You don't forget me. You're still here, right now. Thank You for listening. Now I want to listen to You. Speak Your words of peace to my soul.

Jesus, I Trust In You

Fourth Thursday of Lent

Meditation by Fr. Michael Gaitley, MIC

My daughter, I want to repose in your heart, because many souls have thrown Me out of their hearts today. I have experienced sorrow unto death (866).

Meditation:

Jesus, I'm making a resolution to remember that You're in my heart. Nevertheless, I'm afraid that I'll soon forget that You're there. Well, I'm going to start smiling as soon as I finish this meditation, and that's a sign to You that I love You. People may wonder why I'm smiling, but You'll know for sure. And when I have to stop smiling, or forget to smile, remember that I was smiling for You. And give me gentle reminders to smile for You throughout the day, because I want to cheer You up. At least remember my smile now, and don't be sad, because I love You.

Jesus, I Trust In You

Fourth Friday of Lent
Meditation by Fr. Michael Gaitley, MIC

My daughter, today consider My Sorrowful Passion in all its immensity. Consider it as if it had been undertaken for your sake alone (1761).

Meditation:
Jesus, I'm grateful for all that You suffered for me. Yet I'm afraid I can't fully understand all that Your love endured. Please enlighten me. Help me to know Your greatest suffering. Was it the rejection? I think so. And You endured that for me? Yes. But I caused it, too? Yes, it's true. I've so often subtly rejected You. I'm sorry, Jesus. I'm sorry for drifting from Your love and for not taking time to ponder it. Help me, Lord, to know and experience Your love more deeply. Have compassion on my hardened heart, so I can feel more compassion for You.

Jesus, I Trust In You

Fourth Saturday of Lent

Meditation by Fr. Michael Gaitley, MIC

Encourage the souls with whom you come in contact to trust in My infinite mercy. Oh, how I love those souls who have complete confidence in Me — I will do everything for them (294).

Meditation:

My God, I trust in You, but heal my lack of trust! I want to encourage others to trust in Your mercy, but I myself sometimes feel like I need others to encourage me. Remind me of Your goodness. Help me to experience Your tenderness more deeply. How can I do this? Ah, yes. I'll think about all the good things You've done for me. When I look back on my life, I see that You've helped me through so many difficult times. You've been the best of friends. You were always there for me when I turned to You. Yes, I will encourage others to trust in You, and I will tell them that they will not be disappointed.

Jesus, I Trust In You

My daughter, all your miseries have been consumed in the flame of My love, like a little twig thrown into a roaring fire. By humbling yourself in this way, you draw upon yourself and upon other souls an entire sea of My mercy (178).

Meditation:

Lord Jesus, You know well my constant series of worries and complaints. You know that I love You and desire to trust You more. You know I long to be with You and none other than Yourself. Yet part of me pulls away. Part of me is fearful. Help me to have a childlike confidence in You and Your care for me.

Jesus, I Trust In You

Fifth Monday of Lent

Meditation by Fr. Daniel Cambra, MIC

Your humility draws Me down from My lofty throne, and I unite myself closely with you (1109).

Meditation:

Like a child in the lap of her parent, I desire to rest in the quiet of Your strong arms. Your arms wrap around me, protecting me from the Evil One and all harm. Help me, Lord Jesus, to quietly rest here with You protecting me.

Jesus, I Trust In You

Fifth Tuesday of Lent
Meditation by Fr. Daniel Cambra, MIC

My Jesus, You suffice me for everything else in the world. Although the sufferings are severe, You sustain me. Although the times of loneliness are terrible, You make them sweet for me. Although the weakness is great, You change it into power for me (1655).

Meditation:
Help me, Lord, to fully rely on You, the source of every good. Transform me into Your Love.

Jesus, I Trust In You

Fifth Wednesday of Lent

Meditation by Fr. Daniel Cambra, MIC

Tell me all, My child, hide nothing from Me, because My loving Heart, the Heart of your Best Friend, is listening to you (1486).

Meditation:

Jesus, I trust in You as my Best Friend. You alone do not disappoint me. You do not laugh at my sorrows and worries, which are often trifles. You do not ridicule me, even when I am foolish. How could I live without You? How could I live without Your love in my life?

Jesus, I Trust In You

Fifth Thursday of Lent

Meditation by Fr. Daniel Cambra, MIC

My daughter, know that your ardent love and the compassion you have for Me were a consolation to Me in the Garden [of Olives] (1664).

Meditation:

How is it, Lord, that I should matter so much to You? How could I be worth so much to You? When will I matter so much to myself?

Jesus, I Trust In You

Fifth Friday of Lent

Meditation by Fr. Daniel Cambra, MIC

Look into My Heart and see there the love
and mercy which I have for humankind, and
especially for sinners. Look, and enter into
My Passion (1663).

Meditation:

My sins weigh heavily on my heart when I think
of what I did in ignorance. I feel shame when I
look upon an image of Your love poured forth for
ungrateful humanity. How could I ever so completely reject Your love for me again?

Jesus, I Trust In You

Fifth Saturday of Lent
Meditation by Fr. Daniel Cambra, MIC

I desire that the whole world know My infinite mercy. I desire to grant unimaginable graces to those souls who trust in My mercy (687).

Meditation:
I desire to embrace the whole world for You. I want to tell every soul how much You love them, all at the same time. I want to run up and down the streets, crying out about Your great love for everyone, especially those who are most in need.

Jesus, I Trust In You

I saw Jesus riding on a donkey's foal, and the disciples and a great multitude with branches in their hands joyfully accompanying the Lord Jesus. Some strewed them before His feet where He was riding, while others raised their branches in the air, leaping and jumping before the Lord and not knowing what to do for joy. ... But Jesus was very grave, and the Lord gave me to know how much He was suffering at the time. And at that moment, I saw nothing but only Jesus, whose Heart was saturated with ingratitude (642).

Meditation:

Dearest Jesus, my heart is heavy also. I know that in just a few days You will enter into Your agony. And, even now, You are burdened by the ingratitude and lack of trust of others. But here I am with You, walking somberly beside You, as You ride into the holy city. May my presence here alongside You bring a smile to Your eyes and joy to Your heart, even if only a little.

Jesus, I Trust In You

Monday of Holy Week
Meditation by Fr. Jim McCormack, MIC

Strive for a life of recollection so that you can hear My voice, which is so soft that only recollected souls can hear it (1779).

Meditation:
Lord, as I prepare to enter into Your Passion with You, still my heart, quiet my mind. Help me to hear Your voice speak to my heart Your words of mercy, which my heart so very much longs to hear.

Jesus, I Trust In You

Tuesday of Holy Week
Meditation by Fr. Jim McCormack, MIC

[A particularly intense time of suffering] was an occasion for me to unite myself with Jesus, suffering on the Cross. Beyond that, I was unable to pray (696).

Meditation:
Lord, I am so weak. I tend to run from suffering when it comes my way. But You know my weakness, and You love me anyway. Give me the strength to suffer with You what I must.

Jesus, I Trust In You

Wednesday of Holy Week

Meditation by Fr. Jim McCormack, MIC

Know that a pure soul is humble. When you lower and empty yourself before My majesty, I then pursue you with My graces and make use of My omnipotence to exalt you (576).

Meditation:

O Lord, I know my weaknesses are no obstacle for You. Overcome them and make me a pure and humble vessel for You. May everything I do be done entirely for You and out of love for You.

Jesus, I Trust In You

Holy Thursday

Meditation by Fr. Jim McCormack, MIC

Over the bread and wine He says these words:
"This is My Blood, this is My Body."
Although mysterious, these are words of love.
Then He passes the Cup among His disciples
(1002).

Meditation:

O Lord, how greatly You desire to dine with me,
to give to me Your Body and Blood, that I may
be one with You. In profound gratitude, I now
offer You to the Father as You taught me to do
— for those who so need Your mercy. "Eternal
Father, I offer You the Body and Blood, Soul and
Divinity of Your dearly beloved Son, our Lord
Jesus Christ, in atonement for our sins and those
of the whole world."

Jesus, I Trust In You

Good Friday

Meditation by Fr. Jim McCormack, MIC

During Holy Mass, I saw the Lord Jesus nailed upon the cross amidst great torments. A soft moan issued from His Heart. After some time, He said, **I thirst. I thirst for the salvation of souls. Help Me, My daughter, to save souls. Join your sufferings to My Passion and offer them to the heavenly Father for sinners** (1032).

Meditation:

My Jesus, here I am, with You at the foot of Your Cross. Allow me to quench Your thirst. I offer You my whole being, and I place all my trust in You. May these words be to me like breathing: Jesus, I trust in You!

Jesus, I Trust In You

Holy Saturday

Meditation by Fr. Jim McCormack, MIC

My heart is languishing for God. I desire to become united with Him. A faint fear pierces my soul and at the same time a kind of flame of love sets my heart on fire. Love and suffering are united in my heart (1050).

Meditation:

Mary, in the deepest and darkest moments of my life, when Jesus seems totally absent, help me to remember that I am never alone; you are always here with me to comfort me and to teach me. With your help, dear Mother, I can trust that your Son's absence only appears as such and that I will experience His consoling presence again soon — very soon.

Jesus, I Trust In You

O Jesus, Divine Prisoner of Love, when I consider Your love and how You emptied Yourself for me, my senses fail me. You hide Your inconceivable majesty and lower Yourself to miserable me. O King of Glory, though You hide Your beauty, yet the eye of my soul rends the veil. I see the angelic choirs giving You honor without cease, and all the heavenly Powers praising You without cease, and without cease they are saying: Holy, Holy, Holy (80).

Meditation:
My Jesus, all in heaven glorify You and praise You. I too, little as I am, join in their hymn of praise. Though I cannot fathom all the good You have done for me, loving me, redeeming me, calling me to Yourself, may every beat of my heart sound my gratitude and love.

Jesus, I Trust In You

Easter Monday

Meditation by Fr. Seraphim Michalenko, MIC

My Heart overflows with great mercy for souls, and especially for poor sinners. If only they would understand that I am the best of Fathers to them and that it is for them that the Blood and Water flowed from My Heart as from a fount overflowing with mercy. For them I dwell in the tabernacle as King of Mercy (367).

Meditation:
O Lord, You are indeed so good to me. Draw me ever more closely to You, that I may be united to You.

Jesus, I Trust In You

Easter Tuesday

Meditation by Fr. Seraphim Michalenko, MIC

I perform works of mercy in every soul. The greater the sinner, the greater the right he has to My mercy. My mercy is confirmed in every work of My hands. He who trusts in My mercy will not perish, for all his affairs are Mine (723).

Meditation:

I trust in You, Lord. Work Your mercy in me. Transform this heart of mine by pouring into it Your mercy. And may Your mercy overflow from my heart and pour out upon all those I meet.

Jesus, I Trust In You

Easter Wednesday

Meditation by Fr. Seraphim Michalenko, MIC

Praise the Lord, my soul, for everything, and glorify His mercy, for His goodness is without end. Everything will pass, but His mercy is without limit or end. And although evil will attain its measure, in mercy there is no measure (423).

Meditation:

Your mercy, O Lord, is so vast that I will never exhaust it or deplete it. I resolve to continually draw from Your mercy, this day and all the days of my life, knowing that You will consume my weakness whenever I approach You with a contrite heart.

Jesus, I Trust In You

Easter Thursday
Meditation by Fr. Seraphim Michalenko, MIC

I desire trust from My creatures. Encourage souls to place great trust in My fathomless mercy. Let the weak, sinful soul have no fear to approach Me, for even if it had more sins than there are grains of sand in the world, all would be drowned in the unmeasurable depths of My mercy (1059).

Meditation:
Even though I am weak and sinful, I love You and trust in You. I give to You what really is mine: my troubles, worries, sins, attachments. All of these You can have. O Lord, give me Your love and mercy in exchange.

Jesus, I Trust In You

Easter Friday

Meditation by Fr. Seraphim Michalenko, MIC

My mercy is greater than your sins and those of the entire world. Who can measure the extent of My goodness? For you I descended from heaven to earth; for you I allowed Myself to be nailed to the cross; for you I let My Sacred Heart be pierced with a lance, thus opening wide the source of mercy for you (1485).

Meditation:

Lord, sometimes it seems as if my sins are so great that I cannot get to You. When it seems that my sins are all there is in the world, when it seems that my soul slouches through each day, filled with discouragement, I lift up my gaze to Your merciful, Sacred Heart. Let me praise You as I drink in Your mercy.

Jesus, I Trust In You

Easter Saturday

Meditation by Fr. Seraphim Michalenko, MIC

Be always merciful as I am merciful. Love everyone out of love for Me, even your greatest enemies, so that My mercy may be fully reflected in your heart (1695).

Meditation:

To love my enemies can be difficult, Lord. But I know that to You all things are possible. Guide me in the paths of mercy, and show me how to be merciful to those whom I recoil from or avoid. Being merciful to another may be something as simple as a smile or a kind word, and yet such simple things can be so difficult to do to one I dislike. I beg You for the grace to love them, because You love them, and I love You.

Jesus, I Trust In You

Tell the whole world about My inconceivable mercy. ... On [the Feast of Mercy] the very depths of My tender mercy are open. I pour out a whole ocean of graces upon those souls who approach the Fount of My Mercy. The soul that will go to Confession and receive Holy Communion shall obtain complete forgiveness of sins and punishment. ... Let no soul fear to draw near to Me, even though its sins be as scarlet. My mercy is so great that no mind, be it of man or angel, will be able to fathom it throughout all eternity. Everything that exists has come forth from the very depths of My most tender mercy. ... The Feast of Mercy emerged from My very depths of tenderness. It is My desire that it be solemnly celebrated on the first Sunday after Easter. Mankind will not have peace until it turns to the Fount of My Mercy (699).

Meditation:

May You always be praised for Your greatest attribute: Your mercy. May all souls come to realize and glorify Your mercy, and may I glorify Your mercy all the days of my life, the days of joy and the days of sorrow, and throughout all eternity.

Jesus, I Trust In You

Appendix

Marian Contributors:

Meet the Marian priests who contributed the meditations for *Pausing to Pray: Lenten Meditations for Busy People*.

Fr. Joseph Roesch, MIC, is currently the Second General Councilor for the Marian Fathers in Rome, Italy. He is the co-host for the live EWTN broadcast on Divine Mercy Sunday and the Q&A columnist for *Marian Helper* magazine.

Fr. Donald Calloway, MIC, is the Vocation Director for the Marian Fathers and House Superior of their house in Steubenville, Ohio. He is the author of the bestselling book, *No Turning Back: A Witness to Mercy*. Visit him on his website: www.fathercalloway.com

Fr. Leszek Czeluśniak, MIC, began working in Rwanda in 1989, just two months after he was ordained to the priesthood. He is the Superior of the Marian Fathers' missions in Africa and the Director of CANA, the Marians' center for spiritual development in Kibeho, Rwanda, which is the only Church-approved Marian apparition site in Africa. You can read more about Fr. Leszek on www.kibeho-cana.org.

Fr. Michael Gaitley, MIC, is the Director of the Association of Marian Helpers, a spiritual benefit society with more than 1 million members. He is also the author of the bestselling book, *Consoling the Heart of Jesus*. For more information on his book and Consoling spirituality, visit: www.thedivinemercy.org/chj.

Fr. Daniel Cambra, MIC, is the Provincial Superior of the Marian Fathers of the Immaculate Conception in the U.S. and Argentina. He also travels, speaking on the topics of St. Faustina and Divine Mercy. To see if Fr. Dan is speaking at an event near you, visit: www.thedivinemercy.org/events.

Fr. Jim McCormack, MIC, is the Prefect of Formation and Assistant Novice Master for the Marian Fathers in the United States. He resides at the Marian Scholasticate in Washington, D.C.

Fr. Seraphim Michalenko, MIC, is a world-renowned authority on The Divine Mercy message and the life of St. Faustina. He is the author of the best-selling booklet, *The Divine Mercy Message and Devotion*. He was Vice Postulator for the canonization cause of St. Faustina and instrumental in the translating of the *Diary* from Polish into English.

St. Faustina's Way of the Cross (abbreviated)

I. JESUS IS CONDEMNED TO DEATH.
Do not be surprised if you are sometimes unjustly accused. I Myself first drank this cup of underserved suffering for love of you (289).

II. JESUS TAKES UP HIS CROSS.
Do not be afraid of sufferings; I am with you (151).

III. JESUS FALLS THE FIRST TIME.
My Jesus, despite Your graces, I see and feel all my misery. ... But I do not lose heart. I trust in God's grace, which abounds in the worst misery (606).

IV. JESUS MEETS HIS SORROWFUL MOTHER.
[Mary to St. Faustina] *Do not fear apparent obstacles, but fix your gaze upon the Passion of my Son, and in this way you will be victorious* (449).

V. SIMON OF CYRENE HELPS JESUS CARRY HIS CROSS.
I do not reward for good results but for the patience and hardship undergone for My sake (86).

VI. VERONICA WIPES THE FACE OF JESUS.
Know that whatever good you do to any soul, I accept it as if you had done it to Me (1768).

VII. JESUS FALLS THE SECOND TIME.
Jesus, do not leave me alone in suffering. You know, Lord, how weak I am (1489).

VIII. JESUS CONSOLES THE WOMEN OF JERUSALEM.
O how pleasing to Me is living faith! (1420).

IX. JESUS FALLS THE THIRD TIME.
Do not lose heart in coming for pardon, for I am always ready to forgive you (1488).

X. JESUS IS STRIPPED OF HIS GARMENTS.

My likeness to Jesus must be through suffering and humility (268).

XI. JESUS IS NAILED TO THE CROSS.

My pupil, have great love for those who cause you suffering (1628).

XII. JESUS DIES ON THE CROSS.

All this is for the salvation of souls. Consider well ... what you are doing for their salvation (1184).

XIII. JESUS IS TAKEN DOWN FROM THE CROSS.

Most dear to Me is the soul that strongly believes in My goodness and has complete trust in Me (453).

XIV. JESUS IS LAID IN THE TOMB.

Every soul You have entrusted to me, Jesus, I will try to aid with prayer and sacrifice (245).

Excepts from *St. Faustina's Way of the Cross*, Marian Press, 2002, © Marian Fathers of the Immaculate Conception of the B.V.M.

Examination of Conscience (before Confession)

1. I am the Lord your God, you shall not have other gods before Me.

Do I love with all my heart the Lord who loves me and cares for me? Have I failed to place Him first, or even betrayed Him through occult practices?

2. You shall not take the name of the Lord your God in vain.

Do I revere God's name, or have I taken it lightly, carelessly, or blasphemously, even wishing evil on others? Have I received Him worthily in Holy Communion?

3. Remember to keep holy the Sabbath day.

Do I worship the Lord by taking part in Mass on Sundays and

Holy Days, or have I been indifferent to the Eucharist. Is Sunday my day of rest?

4. Honor your father and your mother.

Have I loved, respected, and obeyed my parents? Do I care for them when they are in need or in old age? Do I forgive them? Am I patient with them?

5. You shall not kill.

Have I loved my neighbor, or have I physically harmed or hastened the death of another through violence, abortion, the morning-after pill, euthanasia, drugs, hatred, or abuse? Do I eat or drink immoderately?

6. and 9. You shall not commit adultery; you shall not covet your neighbor's wife.

Have I been pure and holy in thoughts, words, and actions, or have I been unfaithful to my spouse or desirous of another? Have I been sexually active outside of marriage, or with another of the same sex? Have I indulged in pornography, masturbation, contraception, and other sexual sins?

7. and 10. You shall not steal; you shall not covet your neighbor's goods.

Do I respect other's goods, or have I been envious and greedy, even taking what belongs to another? Have I paid my debts? Have I wasted time at work, at school, or at home? Have money or possessions become my god?

8. You shall not bear false witness against your neighbor.

Have I been honest, or have I lied, gossiped, given false testimony, ruined the good name of another, broken confidentiality, or denied the truth out of pride or hypocrisy?

The Novena to Divine Mercy (short version)

The Chaplet of Divine Mercy featured on the opposite page can be said anytime, but the Lord specifically asked that it be recited as a novena, especially on the nine days before the Feast of Mercy (Divine Mercy Sunday), beginning on Good Friday. He promised, **"By this novena** [of Chaplets] **I will grant every possible grace to souls"** (796). The following are abbreviated intentions for each of the nine days of the Novena. For the full intentions, please see *Diary* entries 1209-1229.

FIRST DAY: **Today bring to Me all mankind, especially all sinners, and immerse them in the ocean of My mercy.**

SECOND DAY: **Today bring to Me the souls of priests and religious, and immerse them in My unfathomable mercy.**

THIRD DAY: **Today bring to Me all devout and faithful souls, and immerse them in the ocean of My mercy.**

FOURTH DAY: **Today bring to Me those who do not believe in God and those who do not yet know Me.**

FIFTH DAY: **Today bring to Me the souls of those who have separated themselves from the Church.**

SIXTH DAY: **Today bring to Me the meek and humble souls and the souls of little children, and immerse them in My mercy.**

SEVENTH DAY: **Today bring to Me the souls who especially venerate and glorify My Mercy and immerse them in My mercy.**

EIGHTH DAY: **Today bring to Me the souls who are detained in purgatory and immerse them in the abyss of My mercy.**

NINTH DAY: **Today bring to Me souls who have become lukewarm, and immerse them in the abyss of My mercy.**